ONE-WAY TICKET

SHORT STORIES

A train is a closed world. Each carriage is like a small room, with windows and doors, but you can't get out when the train is moving. The world outside is far away, and you can forget your home, your work, your friends. On a train you sit with strangers. You don't know anything about them, but you sit next to them for hours, or perhaps days, in the same small room. You can't get away from them.

As the wheels of the train turn, these stories show us three different people. A beautiful young wife – going on holiday with her new husband, through the green hills of England. A carefree young man – travelling across the mountains of Yugoslavia, looking for work. A sensible middle-aged man – travelling north through the forests and lakes of Finland, hoping for a quiet journey.

Three different journeys, three different people – all locked in the closed world of the train . . . where anything can happen.

OXFORD BOOKWORMS LIBRARY

Human Interest

One-Way Ticket

SHORT STORIES

Stage 1 (400 headwords)

Series Editor: Jennifer Bassett
Founder Editor: Tricia Hedge
Activities Editors: Jennifer Bassett and Alison Baxter

To my brothers,
Nick and Rod,
who do a lot of travelling
around Europe by train

JENNIFER BASSETT

One-Way Ticket

SHORT STORIES

OXFORD UNIVERSITY PRESS

OXFORD
UNIVERSITY PRESS

Great Clarendon Street, Oxford OX2 6DP

Oxford University Press is a department of the University of Oxford.
It furthers the University's objective of excellence in research, scholarship,
and education by publishing worldwide in

Oxford New York

Auckland Cape Town Dar es Salaam Hong Kong Karachi
Kuala Lumpur Madrid Melbourne Mexico City Nairobi
New Delhi Shanghai Taipei Toronto

With offices in

Argentina Austria Brazil Chile Czech Republic France Greece
Guatemala Hungary Italy Japan Poland Portugal Singapore
South Korea Switzerland Thailand Turkey Ukraine Vietnam

OXFORD and OXFORD ENGLISH are registered trade marks of
Oxford University Press in the UK and in certain other countries

ISBN 978 0 19 478914 1

A complete recording of this Bookworms edition of
One-Way Ticket is available on audio CD ISBN 978 0 19 478849 6

Printed in China

Illustrated by: Nick Harris

Word count (main text): 5520 words

For more information on the Oxford Bookworms Library,
visit www.oup.com/bookworms

CONTENTS

The Girl with Green Eyes

'Of course,' the man in the brown hat said, 'there are good policemen and there are bad policemen, you know.'

'You're right,' the young man said. 'Yes. That's very true. Isn't it, Julie?' He looked at the young woman next to him.

Julie didn't answer and looked bored. She closed her eyes.

'Julie's my wife,' the young man told the man in the brown hat. 'She doesn't like trains. She always feels ill on trains.'

'Oh yes?' the man in the brown hat said. 'Now my wife – she doesn't like buses. She nearly had an accident on a bus once. It was last year . . . No, no, it wasn't. It was two years ago. I remember now. It was in Manchester.' He told a long, boring story about his wife and a bus in Manchester.

It was a hot day and the train was slow. There were seven people in the carriage. There was the man in the brown hat; the young man and his wife, Julie; a mother and two children; and a tall dark man in an expensive suit.

The young man's name was Bill. He had short brown hair and a happy smile. His wife, Julie, had long red hair

1

*Julie opened her eyes and looked at the back page of the
tall dark man's newspaper.*

and very green eyes – the colour of sea water. They were very beautiful eyes.

The man in the brown hat talked and talked. He had a big red face and a loud voice. He talked to Bill because Bill liked to talk too. The man in the brown hat laughed a lot, and when he laughed, Bill laughed too. Bill liked talking and laughing with people.

The two children were hot and bored. They didn't want to sit down. They wanted to be noisy and run up and down the train.

'Now sit down and be quiet,' their mother said. She was a small woman with a tired face and a tired voice.

'I don't want to sit down,' the little boy said. 'I'm thirsty.'

'Here. Have an orange,' his mother said. She took an orange out of her bag and gave it to him.

'I want an orange too,' the little girl said loudly.

'All right. Here you are,' said her mother. 'Eat it nicely, now.'

The children ate their oranges and were quiet for a minute.

Then the little boy said, 'I want a drink. I'm thirsty.'

The tall dark man took out his newspaper and began to read. Julie opened her eyes and looked at the back page of his newspaper. She read about the weather in Budapest and about the football in Liverpool. She wasn't interested in Budapest and she didn't like football, but she didn't want to listen to Bill and the man in the brown hat. 'Talk, talk, talk,' she thought. 'Bill never stops talking.'

Then suddenly she saw the tall man's eyes over the top of his newspaper. She could not see his mouth, but there was a smile in his eyes. Quickly, she looked down at the newspaper and read about the weather in Budapest again.

The train stopped at Dawlish station and people got on and got off. There was a lot of noise.

'Is this our station?' the little girl asked. She went to the window and looked out.

'No, it isn't. Now sit down,' her mother said.

'We're going to Penzance,' the little girl told Bill. 'For our holidays.'

'Yes,' her mother said. 'My sister's got a little hotel by the sea. We're staying there. It's cheap, you see.'

'Yes,' the man in the brown hat said. 'It's a nice town. I know a man there. He's got a restaurant in King Street. A lot of holiday people go there. He makes a lot of money in the summer.' He laughed loudly. 'Yes,' he said again. 'You can have a nice holiday in Penzance.'

'We're going to St Austell,' Bill said. 'Me and Julie. It's our first holiday. Julie wanted to go to Spain, but I like St Austell. I always go there for my holidays. It's nice in August. You can have a good time there too.'

Julie looked out of the window. 'Where *is* Budapest?'

she thought. 'I want to go there. I want to go to Vienna, to Paris, to Rome, to Athens.' Her green eyes were bored and angry. Through the window she watched the little villages and hills of England.

The man in the brown hat looked at Julie. 'You're right,' he said to Bill. 'You can have a good time on holiday in England. We always go to Brighton, me and the wife. But the weather! We went one year, and it rained every day. Morning, afternoon, and night. It's true. It never stopped raining.' He laughed loudly. 'We nearly went home after the first week.'

Bill laughed too. 'What did you do all day, then?' he asked.

Julie read about the weather in Budapest for the third time. Then she looked at the tall man's hands. They were long, brown hands, very clean. 'Nice hands,' she thought. He wore a very expensive Japanese watch. 'Japan,' she thought. 'I'd like to go to Japan.' She looked up and saw the man's eyes again over the top of his newspaper. This time she did not look away. Green eyes looked into dark brown eyes for a long, slow minute.

After Newton Abbot station the guard came into the carriage to look at their tickets. 'Now then,' he said, 'where are we all going?'

'This train's late,' the man in the brown hat said. 'Twenty minutes late, by my watch.'

Green eyes looked into dark brown eyes
for a long, slow minute.

'Ten minutes,' the guard said. 'That's all.' He smiled at Julie.

The tall dark man put his newspaper down, found his ticket, and gave it to the guard. The guard looked at it.

'You're all right, sir,' he said. 'The boat doesn't leave Plymouth before six o'clock. You've got lots of time.'

The tall man smiled, put his ticket back in his pocket and opened his newspaper again.

Julie didn't look at him. 'A boat,' she thought. 'He's taking a boat from Plymouth. Where's he going?' She looked at him again with her long green eyes.

He read his newspaper and didn't look at her. But his eyes smiled.

The train stopped at Totnes station and more people got on and off.

'Everybody's going on holiday,' Bill said. He laughed. 'It's going to be wonderful. No work for two weeks. It's a nice, quiet town, St Austell. We can stay in bed in the mornings, and sit and talk in the afternoons, and have a drink or two in the evenings. Eh, Julie?' He looked at his wife. 'Are you all right, Julie?'

'Yes, Bill,' she said quietly. 'I'm OK.' She looked out of the window again. The train went more quickly now, and it began to rain. Bill and the man in the brown hat talked and talked. Bill told a long story about two men and a dog, and the man in the brown hat laughed very loudly.

The man in the brown hat laughed very loudly.

'That's a good story,' he said. 'I like that. You tell it very well. Do you know the story about . . .' And he told Bill a story about a Frenchman and a bicycle.

'Why do people laugh at these stories?' Julie thought. 'They're so boring!'

But Bill liked it. Then he told a story about an old woman and a cat, and the man in the brown hat laughed again. 'That's good, too. I don't know. How do you remember them all?'

'Because', Julie thought, 'he tells them every day.'

'I don't understand,' the little girl said suddenly. She looked at Bill. 'Why did the cat die?'

'Shhh. Be quiet,' her mother said. 'Come and eat your sandwiches now.'

'That's all right,' Bill said. 'I like children.'

The man in the brown hat looked at the children's sandwiches. 'Mmm, I'm hungry, too,' he said. 'You can get sandwiches in the restaurant on this train.' He looked at Bill. 'Let's go down to the restaurant, eh? I need a drink too.'

Bill laughed. 'You're right. It's thirsty work, telling stories.'

The two men stood up and left the carriage.

The little girl ate her sandwich and looked at Julie. 'But why did the cat die?' she asked.

'I don't know,' Julie said. 'Perhaps it wanted to die.'

The little girl came and sat next to Julie. 'I like your hair,' she said. 'It's beautiful.' Julie looked down at her and smiled.

For some minutes it was quiet in the carriage. Then the tall dark man opened his bag and took out a book. He put it on the seat next to him, and looked at Julie with a smile. Julie looked back at him, and then down at the book. Famous towns of Italy, she read. Venice, Florence, Rome, Naples. She looked away again, out of the window at the rain. 'Two weeks in St Austell,' she thought. 'With Bill. In the rain.'

After half an hour the two men came back to the carriage. 'There are a lot of people on this train,' Bill said. 'Do you want a sandwich, Julie?'

'No,' she said. 'I'm not hungry. You eat them.'

The train was nearly at Plymouth. Doors opened and people began to move. 'A lot of people get on here,' the man in the brown hat said.

The tall dark man stood up and put his book and his newspaper in his bag. Then he picked up his bag and left the carriage. The train stopped at the station. A lot of people got on the train, and two women and an old man came into the carriage. They had a lot of bags with them. Bill and the man in the brown hat stood up and helped them. One of the women had a big bag of apples. The bag broke and the apples went all over the carriage.

'Oh damn!' she said.

Everybody laughed, and helped her to find the apples. The train moved away from Plymouth station. After a

10

Famous towns of Italy, Julie read. Venice, Florence, Rome, Naples.

minute or two everybody sat down and the woman gave some apples to the children.

'Where's Julie?' Bill said suddenly. 'She's not here.'

'Perhaps she went to the restaurant,' the man in the brown hat said.

'But she wasn't hungry,' Bill said. 'She told me.'

The little girl looked at Bill. 'She got off the train at Plymouth,' she said. 'With the tall dark man. I saw them.'

'Of course she didn't!' Bill said. 'She's on this train. She didn't get off.'

'Yes, she did,' the children's mother said suddenly. 'I saw her too. The tall man waited for her on the platform.'

'He waited for her?' Bill's mouth was open. 'But . . . But he read his newspaper all the time. He didn't talk to Julie. And she never talked to him. They didn't say a word.'

'People don't always need words, young man,' the children's mother said.

'But she's my wife!' Bill's face was red and angry. 'She can't do that!' he said loudly. He stood up. 'I'm going to stop the train.' Everybody looked at him and the two children laughed.

'No,' the man in the brown hat said, 'no, you don't want to do that. Sit down and eat your sandwiches, my friend.'

'But I don't understand. Why did she go? What am I going to do?' Bill's face was very unhappy. After a second or two he sat down again. 'What am I going to do?' he said again.

'Nothing,' the man in the brown hat said. He ate his sandwich slowly. 'Go and have your holiday in St Austell. You can have a good time there. Forget about Julie. Those green eyes, now.' He took out a second sandwich and began to eat it. 'I knew a woman once with green eyes. She gave me a very bad time. No, you want to forget about Julie.'

'*She got off the train at Plymouth. With the tall dark man.*'

South for the Winter

I never stay in one country for a long time. It gets boring. I like to move on, see new places, meet different people. It's a good life, most of the time. When I need money, I get a job. I can do most things – hotel and restaurant work, building work, picking fruit. In Europe you can pick fruit most of the year. You need to be in the right country at the right time, of course. It's not easy work, but the money's not bad.

I like to go south in the winter. Life is easier in the sun, and northern Europe can get very cold in the winter. Last year, 1989 it was, I was in Venice for October. I did some work in a hotel for three weeks, then I began slowly to move south. I always go by train when I can. I like trains. You can walk about on a train, and you meet a lot of people.

I left Venice and went on to Trieste. There I got a cheap ticket for the slow train to Sofia, in Bulgaria. This train goes all down through Yugoslavia, and takes a long time – a day and a half. But that didn't matter to me.

The train left Trieste at nine o'clock on a Thursday morning. There weren't many people on it at first, but at Zagreb more people got on. Two girls went along the corridor, past my carriage. They looked through the door, but they didn't come in. Then an old woman came in, sat down and went to sleep. The two girls came back along the corridor and looked into the carriage again. The train left Zagreb and I looked out of the window for about ten minutes, then I went to sleep too.

When I opened my eyes again, the two girls were in the carriage. They looked friendly, so I said, 'Hullo.'

'Hi!' they said.

'You're American,' I said. 'Or Canadian. Right?'

'American,' the taller girl said. She smiled. 'And you're twenty-three, your name's Tom Walsh, you've got blue eyes, and your mum lives in Burnham-on-Sea, UK. Right?'

'How did you know all that?' I asked.

The second girl laughed. 'She looked at your passport. It's in your coat pocket.'

'Oh. Right.' My coat was on the seat next to me. I took my passport out of my pocket and put it back in my bag. 'Who are you, then?' I asked.

They told me. Melanie and Carol from Los Angeles, USA. They liked Europe, they said. They knew a lot of places – Britain, Holland, Denmark, Germany, France, Spain, Italy, Yugoslavia, Bulgaria, Greece . . .

After the train left Zagreb, I went to sleep.

'I'm going to Bulgaria now,' I said. 'For about a month. Then I'm going south for the winter. Cyprus, or perhaps North Africa.'

'Oh yes?' they said. 'We love Bulgaria. Sofia's a great town. Wonderful.'

'What do you do about money?' I asked.

'Well, you know,' Carol smiled. 'Sometimes we get a little job. This and that. But what about you?'

'Yeah, come on,' Melanie said. 'Tell us about you – Tom Walsh with the blue eyes and the mum in Burnham-on-Sea. What are you doing with your life, hey?'

So I told them. They were nice girls. They were older than me, perhaps twenty-seven or twenty-eight, but I liked them. We talked and laughed for hours. I told them a lot of stories about my life. Some of the stories were true, some weren't. But the girls laughed, and said I was a great guy. I asked them about Bulgaria, because I didn't know the country. They knew Sofia well, they said.

'Hey, Carol,' Melanie said. 'We're staying in Bela Palanka for a day or two. But let's go over to Sofia this weekend and meet Tom there. We can meet him on Saturday night at the Hotel Marmara.'

'Yeah! It's a good hotel,' Carol told me. 'Cheap, but good. What do you think, Tom?'

'Great!' I said. 'Let's do that.'

We talked and laughed for hours.

The train was very slow. We got to Belgrade at six o'clock in the evening, and a lot of people got off. There were only me and the girls in the carriage then. The guard came and looked at our tickets, and went away again.

Carol looked at Melanie. 'Hey, Mel,' she said. 'Why don't you and Tom go along to the restaurant? I'm not hungry, and I want to sleep for an hour.'

'Er . . . Food's very expensive on the train,' I said. 'I haven't got much money just now. I'm going to get a job in Sofia.'

'Oh Tom!' Melanie said. 'Why didn't you tell us? Look, you're a nice guy, right? We're OK for money this week. We can buy you a meal.'

'Of course we can,' Carol said. 'And look, in Sofia, we can take you to the best restaurant in town. It's a great place. We love it.'

What could I say? I was hungry. They had money, I didn't. So Melanie and I went to the restaurant and had a meal. When we came back, Carol was still alone in the carriage. Melanie put her feet on the seat and went to sleep.

At Nis some more people got on the train, and two old men came into our carriage. They looked at Melanie's feet on the seat, and talked in loud voices. Carol laughed, and Melanie opened her eyes and sat up.

'Are we nearly there?' she asked Carol, and looked out of the window.

'Yeah. About half an hour, I think.'

'Why are you getting off at Bela Palanka?' I asked. 'What are you going to do there?'

Melanie smiled. 'Find a cheap hotel, meet people, take a look at the town . . . you know.'

'Just for a day or two,' Carol said.

'But there's nothing there!'

'Oh well, you never know,' Melanie laughed. 'See you in Sofia, right? On Saturday night.'

'The Hotel Marmara, OK? Eight o'clock,' Carol said. 'Don't forget now!'

'OK. Great,' I said. 'See you there.'

The train came into Bela Palanka and stopped. The two girls got off and stood on the platform. They smiled at me through the window. 'Saturday. Eight o'clock,' Melanie shouted.

'OK,' I called. They couldn't hear me because of the noise in the station. They smiled again, picked up their bags and walked away. Nice girls. I'm going to have a great time in Sofia, I thought.

The train left Yugoslavia and crossed into Bulgaria at two o'clock in the morning. Then the train stopped at some village – I don't remember the name. I ate an apple and looked out of the window.

Suddenly there were a lot of policemen on the train. Everybody in the carriage sat up and began to talk.

'Saturday. Eight o'clock,' Melanie shouted.

'What's happening?' I said in Italian to the old man next to me.

'I don't know,' he said in bad Italian. 'Perhaps they're looking for somebody. Look. The police are taking some people off the train.'

Then two policemen came into our carriage, a tall thin one and a short fat one. They looked at everybody carefully . . . and then they looked at me again.

'Come with us, please,' the fat policeman said in English.

'What? Me?' I said. 'Why? What's the matter?'

'And bring your bag with you,' the tall policeman said.

I began to ask a question, but policemen never like questions from young men with long hair. So I stayed quiet, picked up my bag, and went with them.

In the station building there were a lot more policemen, and some people from the train. They were all young people, I saw. Some were afraid, some were bored. The police looked in everybody's bags, and then the people went back to the train.

My two policemen took me to a table. 'Your passport, please,' the fat policeman said, 'and open your bag.'

They looked at my passport and I opened my bag. There was a young policewoman with red hair at the next table. She had a nice face, so I smiled at her and she smiled back.

'Aaah!' the tall policeman said suddenly. All my dirty shirts and clothes were out on the table. The policeman picked up my bag and turned it over. On to the table, out of my bag, fell packet after packet of US American dollars. Nice, new dollars. Fifty-dollar notes in big packets. A lot of money.

Nice, new dollars. Fifty-dollar notes in big packets.
A lot of money.

My mouth opened, and stayed open. I couldn't find my voice. I was suddenly a very interesting person, and a lot of police ran up to our table and stood behind me.

'50,000 . . . 100,000 . . . 150,000 . . . There's 200,000 dollars here,' the tall policeman said. 'What an interesting bag, Mr Tom Walsh!'

I found my voice again quickly. 'But it's not my bag!' I shouted.

There was a big, happy smile on that policeman's face. 'Well,' he said, 'it's got your name on it. Look!'

So I looked, and of course there was my name, and yes of course, it was my bag. So how did 200,000 US dollars get into my bag?

'You cannot bring US dollars into this country,' the fat policeman said. He had very short grey hair and little black eyes. He didn't smile once.

'But I didn't bring them,' I said quickly. 'They're not my dollars. I never saw them before in my life, and —'

There was a lot of noise in the station. I looked out of the window and saw my train. Slowly, it began to move.

'Hey!' I shouted. 'That's my train — '

The tall policeman laughed. It was a great day for him. 'Oh no,' he said. 'You're not getting back on that train. You're staying here with us, in our beautiful country.' He smiled, happily.

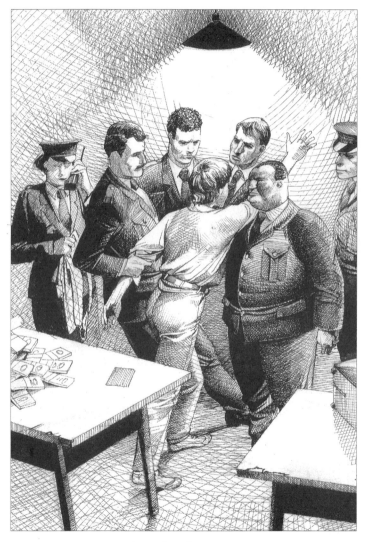

'Hey!' I shouted. 'That's my train — '

So I never got to Sofia on Saturday. I was very unhappy about that. I wanted to have a little talk with Melanie and Carol, ask them one or two questions, you know. *You're a nice guy, Tom. See you in Sofia, OK? Take you to the best restaurant in town.* Yeah. Great.

And I never got down to Cyprus or North Africa that winter. Oh well, I live and learn. It's not an easy life, in prison. But it's warm in winter, and the food's not bad. And I'm meeting some interesting people. There's a man from Georgia, USSR – Boris, his name is. He comes from a place by the Black Sea. He's a great guy. When we get out of here, he and I are going down to Australia . . . Brisbane perhaps, or Sydney. Get a job on a ship, start a new life. Yeah, next year's going to be OK.

Mr Harris and the Night Train

Mr Harris liked trains. He was afraid of aeroplanes, and didn't like buses. But trains – they were big and noisy and exciting. When he was a boy of ten, he liked trains. Now he was a man of fifty, and he still liked trains.

So he was a happy man on the night of the 14th of September. He was on the night train from Helsinki to Oulu in Finland, and he had ten hours in front of him.

'I've got a book and my newspaper,' he thought. 'And there's a good restaurant on the train. And then I've got two weeks' holiday with my Finnish friends in Oulu.'

There weren't many people on the train, and nobody came into Mr Harris's carriage. He was happy about that. Most people on the train slept through the night, but Mr Harris liked to look out of the window, and to read and think.

After dinner in the restaurant Mr Harris came back to his carriage, and sat in his seat next to the window. For an hour or two he watched the trees and lakes of Finland out of the window. Then it began to get dark, so he opened his book and began to read.

At midnight the train stopped at the small station of Otava. Mr Harris looked out of the window, but he saw nobody. The train moved away from the station, into the black night again. Then the door of Mr Harris's carriage opened, and two people came in. A young man and a young woman.

The young woman was angry. She closed the door and shouted at the man: 'Carl! You can't do this to me!' The young man laughed loudly and sat down.

Mr Harris was a small, quiet man. He wore quiet clothes, and he had a quiet voice. He did not like noisy people and loud voices. So he was not pleased. 'Young people are always noisy,' he thought. 'Why can't they talk quietly?'

He put his book down and closed his eyes. But he could not sleep because the two young people didn't stop talking.

The young woman sat down and said in a quieter voice: 'Carl, you're my brother and I love you, but please listen to me. You can't take my diamond necklace. Give it back to me now. Please!'

Carl smiled. 'No, Elena,' he said. 'I'm going back to Russia soon, and I'm taking your diamonds with me.' He took off his hat and put it on the seat. 'Elena, listen. You have a rich husband, but I – I have no money. I have nothing! How can I live without money? You can't give me money, so I need your diamonds, little sister.'

The young man laughed loudly and sat down.

Mr Harris looked at the young woman. She was small, with black hair and dark eyes. Her face was white and afraid. Mr Harris began to feel sorry for Elena. She and her brother didn't look at him once. 'Can't they see me?' he thought.

'Carl,' Elena said. Her voice was very quiet now, and Mr Harris listened carefully. 'You came to dinner at our house tonight, and you went to my room and took my diamond necklace. How could you do that to me? My husband gave the diamonds to me. They were his mother's diamonds before that. He's going to be very, very angry – and I'm afraid of him.'

Her brother laughed. He put his hand in his pocket, then took it out again and opened it slowly. The diamond necklace in his hand was very beautiful. Mr Harris stared at it. For a minute or two nobody moved and it was quiet in the carriage. There was only the noise of the train, and it went quickly on through the dark cold night.

Mr Harris opened his book again, but he didn't read it. He watched Carl's face, with its hungry eyes and its cold smile.

'What beautiful, beautiful diamonds!' Carl said. 'I can get a lot of money for these.'

'Give them back to me, Carl,' Elena whispered. 'My husband's going to kill me. You're my brother . . . Please help me. Please!'

The diamond necklace in Carl's hand was very beautiful.

Carl laughed again, and Mr Harris wanted to hit him. 'Go home, little sister,' Carl said. 'I'm not going to give the diamonds back to you. Go home to your angry husband.'

Suddenly there was a knife in the young woman's hand. A long, bright knife. Mr Harris watched with his mouth open. He couldn't speak or move.

'Give the diamonds back to me!' Elena cried. 'Or I'm going to kill you!' Her hand on the knife was white.

Carl laughed and laughed. 'What a sister!' he said. 'What a kind, sweet sister! No, they're my diamonds now. Put your knife away, little sister.'

But the knife in the white hand moved quickly: up, then down. There was a long, terrible cry, and Carl's body fell slowly on to the seat. The colour of the seat began to change to red, and the diamond necklace fell from Carl's hand on to the floor.

Elena's face was white. 'Oh no!' she whispered. 'Carl! Come back . . . come back! I didn't want to kill you!' But Carl didn't answer, and the red blood ran slowly over the floor. Elena put her head in her hands, and again in the carriage there was a long, terrible cry.

Mr Harris's face was white too. He opened his mouth, but he couldn't speak. He stood up, and carefully moved to the door. The young woman was quiet now. She didn't move or look up at Mr Harris.

There was a long, terrible cry, and Carl's body fell slowly on to the seat.

In the corridor, Mr Harris ran. The guard was at the back of the train and Mr Harris got there in half a minute.

'Quickly!' Mr Harris said. 'Come quickly! An accident . . . a young woman . . . oh dear! Her brother is . . . is dead!'

The guard ran with Mr Harris back to the carriage. Mr Harris opened the door and they went inside.

The guard ran with Mr Harris back to the carriage.

There was no dead body of a young man. There was no young woman . . . no blood, no knife, no diamond necklace. Only Mr Harris's bags and his hat and coat.

The guard looked at Mr Harris, and Mr Harris looked at him.

'But . . .' Mr Harris began. 'But they were here! I saw them! She . . . the young woman . . . She had a knife and she . . . she killed her brother.'

'A knife, you say?' the guard asked.

'Yes,' Mr Harris said quickly. 'A long knife, and her brother took her diamonds, so she — '

'Ah! Diamonds!' the guard said. 'Was the young woman's name Elena?' he asked.

'Yes, it was!' Mr Harris said. 'How do you know that? Do you . . . Do you know her?'

'Yes — and no,' the guard said slowly. He thought for a minute, then looked at Mr Harris. 'Elena di Saronelli,' he said. 'She had dark eyes and black hair. Very beautiful. She was half-Italian, half-Finnish. Her brother was a half-brother. They had the same father, but *his* mother was Russian, I think.'

'Was? Had?' Mr Harris stared at the guard. 'But she . . . Elena . . . she's alive! And where is she?'

'Oh no,' said the guard. 'Elena di Saronelli died about eighty years ago. After she killed her brother with a knife, she jumped off the train, and died at once. It was near

35

here, I think.' He looked out of the window, into the night.

Mr Harris's face was very white again. 'Eighty years ago!' he whispered. 'What are you saying? Were she and her brother . . . But I saw them!'

'Yes, that's right,' the guard said. 'You saw them, but they're not alive. They're ghosts. They often come on the night train at this time in September. *I* never see them, but somebody saw them last year. A man and his wife. They were very unhappy about it. But what can I do? I can't stop Elena and Carl coming on the train.'

The guard looked at Mr Harris's white face. 'You need a drink,' he said. 'Come and have a vodka with me.'

Mr Harris didn't usually drink vodka, but he felt afraid. When he closed his eyes, he could see again Elena's long knife and could hear her terrible cry. So he went with the guard to the back of the train.

After the vodka, Mr Harris felt better. He didn't want to sleep, and the guard was happy to talk. So Mr Harris stayed with the guard and didn't go back to his carriage.

'Yes,' the guard said, 'it's a famous story. I don't remember it all. It happened a long time ago, of course. Elena's father was a famous man here in Finland. He was very rich once, but he had three or four wives and about eight children. And he liked the good things of life. So there wasn't much money for the children. Carl, the oldest

'Yes,' the guard said, 'it's a famous story.'

son, was a bad man, people say. He wanted an easy life, and money in his hand all the time.'

The train hurried on to Oulu through the black night, and the guard drank some more vodka. 'Now, Elena,' he said. 'She didn't have an easy life with those three difficult men – her father, her brother, her husband. One year she visited her mother's family in Italy, and there she met her husband, di Saronelli. He was rich, but he wasn't a kind man. They came back to Finland, and Carl often visited their house. He wanted money from his sister's rich husband. Elena loved her brother, and gave him some money. But di Saronelli didn't like Carl and was angry with Elena. He stopped giving her money, and after that . . . well, you know the story now.'

'Yes,' Mr Harris said. 'Poor, unhappy Elena.'

Mr Harris stayed with his friends in Oulu for two weeks. They were quiet weeks, and Mr Harris had a good holiday. But he took the bus back to Helsinki. The bus was slow, and there were a lot of people on it, but Mr Harris was very happy. He didn't want to take the night train across Finland again.

GLOSSARY

blood the red liquid in a person's body

boat a small ship

bored not interested

boring not interesting

bright not dark; giving a lot of light

bus a very big car for many people to travel in

buy to get something with money

carriage a 'room' on a train

clean (*adj*) not dirty

clothes things you wear, e.g. dresses, shirts, trousers

corridor the long narrow place on a train with doors to the
    carriages

damn a word to show that you are angry

diamond a beautiful, very expensive, bright stone; women
    wear diamonds in rings, necklaces, etc

fall (past tense **fell**) to move suddenly from a high place to a
    low place

floor the 'ground' in a room; you walk on a floor

fruit apples, oranges, bananas, etc.

ghost a dead person that living people think they can see

great very good; wonderful

guard a man who works on a train

guy a man

Hi hello

holiday days or weeks when people do not go to work

hurry (*v*) to move or do something very quickly

job work that you do for money

jump (*v*) to move quickly with both feet off the ground

kind (*adj*) friendly; good to other people

lake a big area of water, with land all round it

life the time when you are alive, not dead

loud not quiet; with a lot of noise

meal food that you eat at a certain time (e.g. breakfast, dinner)

necklace something beautiful that women wear round their necks

newspaper you read a newspaper to know what is happening in the world

page one piece of paper in a book or newspaper

pick up to take something in the hand

platform trains stop next to a platform in a station, and people get off the train onto the platform

police people who look for bad people and send them to prison

poor when you say 'poor', you are feeling sorry for somebody

prison a big building for bad people; they live there and cannot leave

restaurant a place where you can buy a meal and eat it

seat a 'chair' on a train

shout (*v*) to speak or cry very loudly and strongly

sir when you don't know a man's name, you can call him 'sir'

stare (*v*) to look at someone or something for a long time

station trains stop at stations for people to get on or off

sweet (of people) very nice

terrible something terrible makes you very afraid or unhappy

unhappy not happy

vodka a very strong cold drink

voice you talk with your voice

whisper (*v*) to speak very, very quietly

yeah yes

One-Way Ticket

SHORT STORIES

ACTIVITIES

Before Reading

1 What is a one-way ticket? Do you know, or can you guess?

1 It's for a journey from A to B and B to A.

2 It's for a journey from A to B.

3 It's for a journey from A to B, B to C, and C to A.

2 Read the introduction on the first page of the book, and the back cover. What do you know or what can you guess about these stories? Tick one box for each sentence.

The Girl with Green Eyes   YES   NO

1 The beautiful young wife is the girl with
   green eyes.   ☐   ☐

2 She is going on holiday in Finland.   ☐   ☐

3 She loses something important on the train.   ☐   ☐

4 She gets angry with her new husband.   ☐   ☐

5 Her husband has an accident on the train.   ☐   ☐

South for the Winter   YES   NO

6 Tom Walsh is looking for work.   ☐   ☐

7 He is in a hurry.   ☐   ☐

8 He makes some new friends on the train.   ☐   ☐

9 Something bad happens to him.   ☐   ☐

10 He learns something about life.   ☐   ☐

Mr Harris and the Night Train	YES	NO
11 Mr Harris is a middle-aged man.	☐	☐
12 He is going to visit his mother.	☐	☐
13 He wants to meet people and talk to them on his journey.	☐	☐
14 He sleeps all through the night.	☐	☐
15 He sees something terrible on the train.	☐	☐

3 **What is going to happen in these stories? Can you guess? Tick one box for each sentence.**

Story 1: The Girl with Green Eyes
Story 2: South for the Winter
Story 3: Mr Harris and the Night Train

	1	2	3
1 Someone dies.	☐	☐	☐
2 Someone falls in love.	☐	☐	☐
3 Someone goes to prison.	☐	☐	☐
4 Someone gets a lot of money.	☐	☐	☐
5 Someone loses something.	☐	☐	☐
6 Someone jumps off the train.	☐	☐	☐

While Reading

Read *The Girl with Green Eyes*. Who did what in this story? How many true sentences can you make?

The man in the brown hat	read a newspaper.
Julie	talked a lot.
Bill	smiled but never spoke.
The mother	got off the train at Plymouth.
The little girl	went to the restaurant.
The little boy	saw Julie on the platform.
The tall dark man	was bored.

Here are some untrue sentences about the story. Change them into true sentences.

1 The man in the brown hat was an interesting man.
2 The tall dark man read the back page of Julie's newspaper.
3 Nobody got on the train at Plymouth.
4 Julie said goodbye to Bill when she got off the train.
5 Bill was very happy when Julie left.
6 The man in the brown hat wanted Bill to remember Julie.

Read *South for the Winter*. Then put these sentences into the right order, to make a short paragraph.

1 They took all his clothes out of the bag,
2 and so he went to prison.
3 Tom didn't know anything about this money,
4 two policemen came into Tom's carriage.
5 but the dollars were in his bag,
6 A lot of US dollars fell out on to the table.
7 They told Tom to go with them into the station building,
8 and then picked it up and turned it over.
9 When the train stopped at a village,
10 and to bring his bag with him.

Read *Mr Harris and the Night Train*. Choose the best question-word for these questions, and then answer them.

Who / What / Why

1 . . . did Mr Harris do after dinner?
2 . . . came into Mr Harris's carriage after Otava?
3 . . . did Carl want Elena's diamond necklace?
4 . . . gave the diamonds to Elena?
5 . . . did Carl do when Elena took out a knife?
6 . . . was in the carriage when Mr Harris came back?
7 . . . never saw the ghosts of Carl and Elena?
8 . . . did Mr Harris take the bus back to Helsinki?

After Reading

1 Complete this crossword with words from the stories.

ACROSS

2 Elena di Saronelli was one of these. (5)

4 Bill's stories were not interesting; they were _____. (6)

8 When you wait for a train, you stand on this. (8)

9 A 'room' on a train. (8)

10 You sit on this on a train. (4)

11 Tom went to this place for the winter. (6)

12 Julie was _____ with Bill. (5)

DOWN

1 You walk along this on a train. (8)

3 A train stops at this. (7)

5 This man works on a train. (5)

6 Elena killed Carl with this. (5)

7 Julie and the tall dark man talked with these. (4)

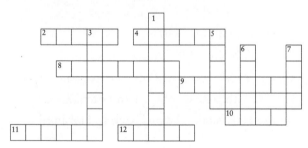

2 In *The Girl with Green Eyes*, Julie and the tall dark man did not talk, but here is a 'conversation' between their eyes, in the wrong order. Write it out in the correct order and put in the speakers' names. The tall dark man speaks first (number 7).

1 _____ 'Of course you can. Bill is more interested in his stories than in his beautiful wife. And you are beautiful, Julie. You have the most wonderful eyes.'

2 _____ 'I can't do that! What about Bill?'

3 _____ 'No buts. Come with me to Italy. You can be happy with me. Don't you want to be happy?'

4 _____ 'How wonderful! I'd love to go to Italy. But I'm going to St Austell.'

5 _____ 'Say nothing. That's the best way. Just get off the train at Plymouth after me.'

6 _____ 'Yes, that's true. I *am* bored. But he's my husband, and I can't just leave him . . . can I?'

7 _____ 'Do you see my book about Italy? I'm going to visit these four famous cities.'

8 _____ 'All right. Wait for me on the platform!'

9 _____ 'Well, what about him? You don't like him. You're bored with him.'

10 _____ 'OK, I have wonderful eyes, but . . .'

11 _____ 'St Austell's a boring town. Come with me to Italy.'

12 _____ 'Yes. Yes, I do. But what do I say to Bill?'

3 Tom (in *South for the Winter*) writes a letter home to his mother, but he gets a lot of things wrong. Find his mistakes and correct them. And he forgets to say one important thing. What is it?

Dear Mum

I left Italy last autumn and came north by bus. I'm staying here in Cyprus for the summer. I've got a job in a hotel, and I've got lots of money. So life is easy. Next year, I'm going to America with an old friend – his name's Ivan. We're going to start a new life in Los Angeles. Hope you're well. Give my love to Burnham-on-Sea!

Love from Tom

4 When Mr Harris arrived in Oulu, his friend met him at the station. Complete their conversation with these words. (Use one word for each gap.)

blood, bus, but, diamond, happened, journey, killed, knows, man, nothing, right, sister's, sleep, terrible, there, train, true, why

FRIEND: Mr Harris, how nice to see you! Did you have a good _____?

MR HARRIS: Well, not very good. I didn't _____ all night.

FRIEND: Oh, that's bad. But _____ couldn't you sleep?

MR HARRIS: Because _____ were two ghosts in my carriage.

FRIEND: Ghosts? How exciting! What _____?

MR HARRIS: It was a young _____ and his sister. He had a
_____ necklace, but it was his _____ necklace and she
wanted it back. And in the end she _____ her brother
with a knife. It was _____! There was _____ everywhere
– I saw it! I ran to get the guard, _____ when we came
back, there was _____ there.

FRIEND: Ah, wait a minute. It was Elena di Saronelli and
her brother Carl, yes?

MR HARRIS: That's _____, but how did you know?

FRIEND: Oh, everyone in Finland _____ that story.

MR HARRIS: But is it _____?

FRIEND: Of course it is. You saw their ghosts, didn't you?
Well, well, how exciting! And when you take the _____
back to Helsinki . . .

MR HARRIS: Oh no, I'm going back to Helsinki by _____.
No more ghosts for me, thank you!

5 **What do you think about ghosts? Do you agree (A) or
disagree (D) with these sentences?**

1 There *are* ghosts.

2 There *aren't* ghosts.

3 Some people *can* see ghosts, but other people can't see
them.

4 Perhaps there are ghosts, and perhaps there aren't; we
just don't know.

6 **Here is a new illustration for one of the stories. Find the best place for it, and answer these questions.**

The picture goes on page _____, in the story _____.
1 Who is the girl in the picture?
2 What is she doing, and why is she doing it?
3 Where are the other two people in this story?

Now write a caption for the illustration.

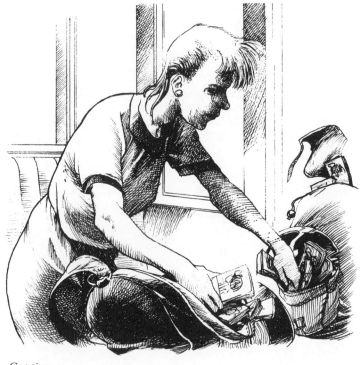

Caption: _____

7 **What did you think about the people in these stories? Were the men nicer people than the women? Did you feel sorry for anybody? Choose some names, and complete some of these sentences.**

Julie / Bill / the tall dark man / the man in the brown hat
Tom / Melanie / Carol
Mr Harris / Elena / Carl

1 I feel sorry for _____ because _____.
2 I think _____ was a nice person but _____.
3 _____ was right to _____.
4 _____ was wrong to _____.
5 I think _____ did a very bad thing.
6 _____ did the worst thing.

8 **Here are some new titles for the three stories. Which titles go with which stories? Some are better titles than others. Can you say why?**

Saturday Night in Sofia   Love Before Plymouth
A Man Called Bill   Happy Days in Finland
Murder in the Night   Green Eyes, Brown Eyes
A Loving Sister   Don't Talk to Strangers
A Holiday in St Austell   The Ghost Train
The American Girls   An Easy Winter

ABOUT THE AUTHOR

Jennifer Bassett has worked in English Language Teaching since 1972. She has been a teacher, teacher trainer, editor, and materials writer, and has taught in England, Greece, Spain, and Portugal. She is the current Series Editor of the Oxford Bookworms Library, and has written several other stories for the series, including *The Phantom of the Opera* and *The President's Murderer* (both at Stage 1). She lives and works in Devonshire, in the south-west of England.

The stories in *One-Way Ticket* were inspired by her many train journeys across Europe. She loves the 'closed world' of the train, and over the years has had many interesting, and sometimes surprising, conversations with other travellers. 'People tell you their life stories on trains,' she says, 'because they know they will never see you again.'

OXFORD BOOKWORMS LIBRARY

Classics • Crime & Mystery • Factfiles • Fantasy & Horror
Human Interest • Playscripts • Thriller & Adventure
True Stories • World Stories

The OXFORD BOOKWORMS LIBRARY provides enjoyable reading in English, with a wide range of classic and modern fiction, non-fiction, and plays. It includes original and adapted texts in seven carefully graded language stages, which take learners from beginner to advanced level. An overview is given on the next pages.

All Stage 1 titles are available as audio recordings, as well as over eighty other titles from Starter to Stage 6. All Starters and many titles at Stages 1 to 4 are specially recommended for younger learners. Every Bookworm is illustrated, and Starters and Factfiles have full-colour illustrations.

The OXFORD BOOKWORMS LIBRARY also offers extensive support. Each book contains an introduction to the story, notes about the author, a glossary, and activities. Additional resources include tests and worksheets, and answers for these and for the activities in the books. There is advice on running a class library, using audio recordings, and the many ways of using Oxford Bookworms in reading programmes. Resource materials are available on the website <www.oup.com/bookworms>.

The *Oxford Bookworms Collection* is a series for advanced learners. It consists of volumes of short stories by well-known authors, both classic and modern. Texts are not abridged or adapted in any way, but carefully selected to be accessible to the advanced student.

You can find details and a full list of titles in the *Oxford Bookworms Library Catalogue* and *Oxford English Language Teaching Catalogues*, and on the website <www.oup.com/bookworms>.

THE OXFORD BOOKWORMS LIBRARY
GRADING AND SAMPLE EXTRACTS

STARTER • 250 HEADWORDS

present simple – present continuous – imperative –
can/cannot, must – *going to* (future) – simple gerunds ...

Her phone is ringing – but where is it?

Sally gets out of bed and looks in her bag. No phone. She looks under the bed. No phone. Then she looks behind the door. There is her phone. Sally picks up her phone and answers it. *Sally's Phone*

STAGE 1 • 400 HEADWORDS

... past simple – coordination with *and*, *but*, *or* –
subordination with *before*, *after*, *when*, *because*, *so* ...

I knew him in Persia. He was a famous builder and I worked with him there. For a time I was his friend, but not for long. When he came to Paris, I came after him – I wanted to watch him. He was a very clever, very dangerous man. *The Phantom of the Opera*

STAGE 2 • 700 HEADWORDS

... present perfect – *will* (future) – *(don't) have to, must not, could* –
comparison of adjectives – simple *if* clauses – past continuous –
tag questions – *ask/tell* + infinitive ...

While I was writing these words in my diary, I decided what to do. I must try to escape. I shall try to get down the wall outside. The window is high above the ground, but I have to try. I shall take some of the gold with me – if I escape, perhaps it will be helpful later. *Dracula*

STAGE 3 • 1000 HEADWORDS

... should, may – present perfect continuous – *used to* – past perfect –
causative – relative clauses – indirect statements ...

Of course, it was most important that no one should see
Colin, Mary, or Dickon entering the secret garden. So Colin
gave orders to the gardeners that they must all keep away
from that part of the garden in future. *The Secret Garden*

STAGE 4 • 1400 HEADWORDS

... past perfect continuous – passive (simple forms) –
would conditional clauses – indirect questions –
relatives with *where/when* – gerunds after prepositions/phrases ...

I was glad. Now Hyde could not show his face to the world
again. If he did, every honest man in London would be proud
to report him to the police. *Dr Jekyll and Mr Hyde*

STAGE 5 • 1800 HEADWORDS

... future continuous – future perfect –
passive (modals, continuous forms) –
would have conditional clauses – modals + perfect infinitive ...

If he had spoken Estella's name, I would have hit him. I was so
angry with him, and so depressed about my future, that I could
not eat the breakfast. Instead I went straight to the old house.
Great Expectations

STAGE 6 • 2500 HEADWORDS

... passive (infinitives, gerunds) – advanced modal meanings –
clauses of concession, condition

When I stepped up to the piano, I was confident. It was as if I
knew that the prodigy side of me really did exist. And when I
started to play, I was so caught up in how lovely I looked that
I didn't worry how I would sound. *The Joy Luck Club*

The Lottery Winner

ROSEMARY BORDER

Everybody wants to win the lottery. A million pounds, perhaps five million, even ten million. How wonderful! Emma Carter buys a ticket for the lottery every week, and puts the ticket carefully in her bag. She is seventy-three years old and does not have much money. She would like to visit her son in Australia, but aeroplane tickets are very expensive.

Jason Williams buys lottery tickets every week too. But he is not a very nice young man. He steals things. He hits old ladies in the street, snatches their bags and runs away . . .

Sister Love and Other Crime Stories

JOHN ESCOTT

Some sisters are good friends, some are not. Sometimes there is more hate in a family than there is love. Karin is beautiful and has lots of men friends, but she can be very unkind to her sister Marcia. Perhaps when they were small, there was love between them, but that was a long time ago.

They say that everybody has one crime in them. Perhaps they only take an umbrella that does not belong to them. Perhaps they steal from a shop, perhaps they get angry and hit someone, perhaps they kill . . .